The Girl in the GOLD DRESS

Written by
Christine Paik
Illustrated by
Jung Lin Park

Design by Bryony van der Merwe
Library of Congress Cataloguing-in-Publication data is available upon request.

ISBN 978-1-954109-10-0 (Paperback)
978-1-954109-11-7 (Hardback)
978-1-954109-12-4 (Ebook)

First Edition: May 2021

imagilore

PUBLISHING

IMAGILORE PUBLISHING
www.imagilore.com

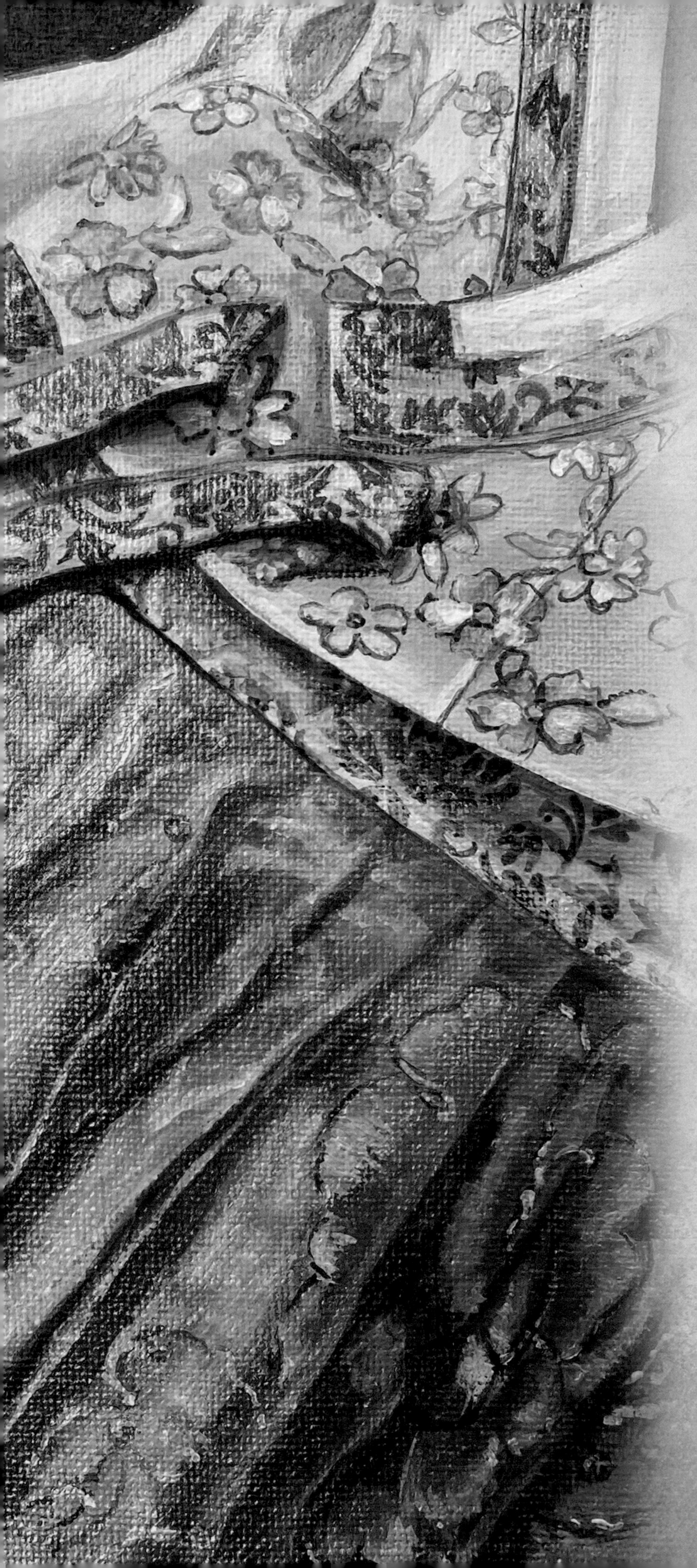

Dedication

To my husband Gene
and my children Sydney
and Isaiah. I love doing
life with you.

And to our Korean
mothers and
grandmothers
who struggled so we
didn't have to.

"What if no one likes my dress?"

Hannah wondered nervously. The brightly colored hanbok dress she was wearing suddenly seemed way too fancy. The material felt itchy and uncomfortable. She felt a drop of sweat forming on her forehead.

"Nonsense!" Mom said cheerfully from the driver's seat.

"You look beautiful! Like a Korean princess."

"A Korean princess never had to perform in her school's talent show," Hannah groaned. She regretted signing up for the Bluff Creek Elementary student showcase. Hannah thought back to the dress rehearsal the night before.

She had watched from backstage as the other students each took the stage to practice.

Her best friend Layla had performed a sassy jazz dance number.

Hannah envied her confidence.

Reena sang a song from Frozen.

Hannah hummed along to try to make the butterflies in her stomach go away.

Nolan strummed a song he'd written about his naughty new puppy. The kids backstage clapped and laughed.

Hannah twisted the fabric of her dress between trembling fingers.

The full skirt of her dress caught under her foot and she tripped as she walked on stage. She heard a few kids snicker. Her cheeks turned red, but she tried to ignore them.

She stood holding her two flower fans, pink feather tips raised in the air, then nodded at the emcee to play her Korean traditional music.

The first crash of the gong on the speakers made everybody jump. **"What was that?! That sounds so weird!"** she heard someone yell.

Hannah froze with her fans mid-air. Everyone sat silently watching her. From somewhere in the back, she heard a giggle. She ran off the stage without rehearsing her dance.

Later, when mom had asked, "How did the rehearsal go?" Hannah had mumbled, "Fine." She couldn't bring herself to explain what really happened.

Remembering, she looked down in shame.

Why had she let her mom convince her to perform a traditional fan dance wearing a hanbok dress? It was too different. Too Korean.

What if the other kids hated it? They'd laughed at the music. They were probably laughing at her dress, too. She traced the gold pattern in her skirt.

"What's wrong, hon?" mom asked gently. She always knew when something was bothering Hannah.

"I don't think I can do this," she whispered as she hung her head. **"I'm too embarrassed to wear this and dance on stage."**

"Did you know, your hanbok has a story?" mom asked, smiling.

"Mom, I already know the story. We got it during our trip to South Korea for my 10th birthday. It was after we walked around grandpa's old neighborhood in Seoul."

"Yes, but did you know the marketplace where we bought the hanbok was the **exact spot** your great-grandma, your grandpa's mom, used to sell hanboks **over 60 years ago?"**

"Really?
She sold hanboks?
I didn't know that."

"Well, not hanboks exactly. She sold **special material** used to make hanboks. She had the best and brightest fabrics for sale. Imagine all the colors of the rainbow. Thick smooth satin. Thin crinkly silk. Coarse linens. Every day, she would lay out the material to catch the eye of people passing by. And she always made sure to wear the prettiest hanboks to attract more customers."

"But her life wasn't always so pretty."

Your great-grandma lived during the Korean War and had to work very hard to survive. She had five children, and she lost her husband during the war, so she had to be brave for her family. Every day the fighting grew closer.

The bombs rumbled like thunder in the distance.

Sometimes the walls of their small home shook.

She was afraid! She knew she needed to get her children to safety, out of North Korea, and she knew she HAD to bring her fabrics with her. It was the only way she could make money and provide for her family. But how? If she was going to escape with her children, she couldn't carry many bags with her. She couldn't risk losing her belongings and her children in the crowds.

The night before their escape, your great-grandma was too nervous to sleep. She woke her children up extra early to get ready for the trip.

As her children watched, she started wrapping the fabrics one by one around parts of her body.

First, the **green one** with swirls went around her left leg. Next, the **purple one** with butterflies around her right leg. The **red one** with **gold scrolls** she tied around her waist. The **light blue one** with silver flowers went around her left arm, and the multi-colored rainbow one on her right arm.

She hand-picked only the finest, most expensive fabrics to take. She placed her favorite one, a shimmering peach and gold fabric she had used for her wedding hanbok, on top. She wrapped them around and around, until she could barely move! She somehow managed to put on a coat over all that material she was wearing! Her children laughed. They thought she looked silly, like a snowman! They didn't realize the fabrics would eventually mean food and a home for them. They had nothing else to help them start their new life.

It was a sad day for all of them. They would never see their home in North Korea again. But there was no time for tears. Great-grandma knew that there was nothing to be gained from looking back. She always said that **life is full of moments to step forward**. This was one of those moments.

The train was packed with people desperate to escape the war.

Some people even climbed onto the roof.

Great-grandma
and her children
were lucky to
squeeze into a
compartment.

She was so hot, wrapped in all those fabrics. She couldn't even use the bathroom!

The train ride south felt like the longest trip great-grandma had ever taken. She stood there for hours, sweating, worrying, and hoping, while all around her, people pushed and cried and yelled over the noise.

She kept looking around for her children, and counting each one, to make sure they didn't get lost. One by one her children fell asleep, but your great-grandma didn't dare close her eyes.

She tried not to think about how uncomfortable she was. She tried not to think about how scared she was. Instead, she thought to herself, **"Life is full of moments to step forward."**

She spent the rest of the trip imagining the most beautiful hanboks that she would create in her new home.

"The one she spent the most time thinking about during the train ride, was made with the last piece of fabric she had wrapped around her body. The skirt was a shimmery peach and gold. The tiny green and pink flowers on the cream jacket were each sewn by hand. The ribbons had..."

"Wait a minute—"

Hannah interrupted, looking down at her own hanbok,

"that sounds a lot like the one I'm wearing right now!

How is that possible?"

Mom leaned closer. "Well, after they escaped to South Korea, your great-grandma sold most of the fabrics that she brought with her. She eventually saved enough to start a small hanbok fabric business in Seoul.

But she never sold her favorite fabric, the peach and gold one that she brought with her on the train so many years ago.

It was too precious."

"Eventually, another lady took over her business, and your great-grandma told her she was leaving South Korea and moving to America. But before she left, she made that hanbok she had dreamed about out of the special peach and gold material. She told the new owner to never sell the hanbok to anyone until the right person came along. Your great-grandma handed her an envelope, **made a secret wish**, and said, '**This is how you'll know.**'"

"What was in the envelope?

What did it say?

What did she wish?" Hannah cried.

She had forgotten all about the talent show.

"The lady promised your great-grandma she would keep the hanbok, but the right person never came. After many years, she passed the shop on to her own daughter, as well as the **mysterious hanbok and envelope.**"

"Wait—so the shop we went to in South Korea..."

"... is that same shop. And your hanbok..."

"...is the same hanbok?" Hannah whispered.

"The very same." Mom patted Hannah's hand and smiled.

Hannah remembered how she had been so drawn to the beautiful peach and gold hanbok without knowing why, and how she had begged her mom to get it for her.

"How...how did they know to give it to me?

And how did great-grandma know what to do with the hanbok before I was born?"

"Your great-grandma named you when you were born," mom explained. "Your American name is Hannah, but your Korean name is Geum Chun. It means gold dress. We thought it was an unusual name, but we liked it."

"The envelope contained a letter explaining that if a Korean-American girl with the name Geum Chun ever came to the store, the hanbok should be given to her.

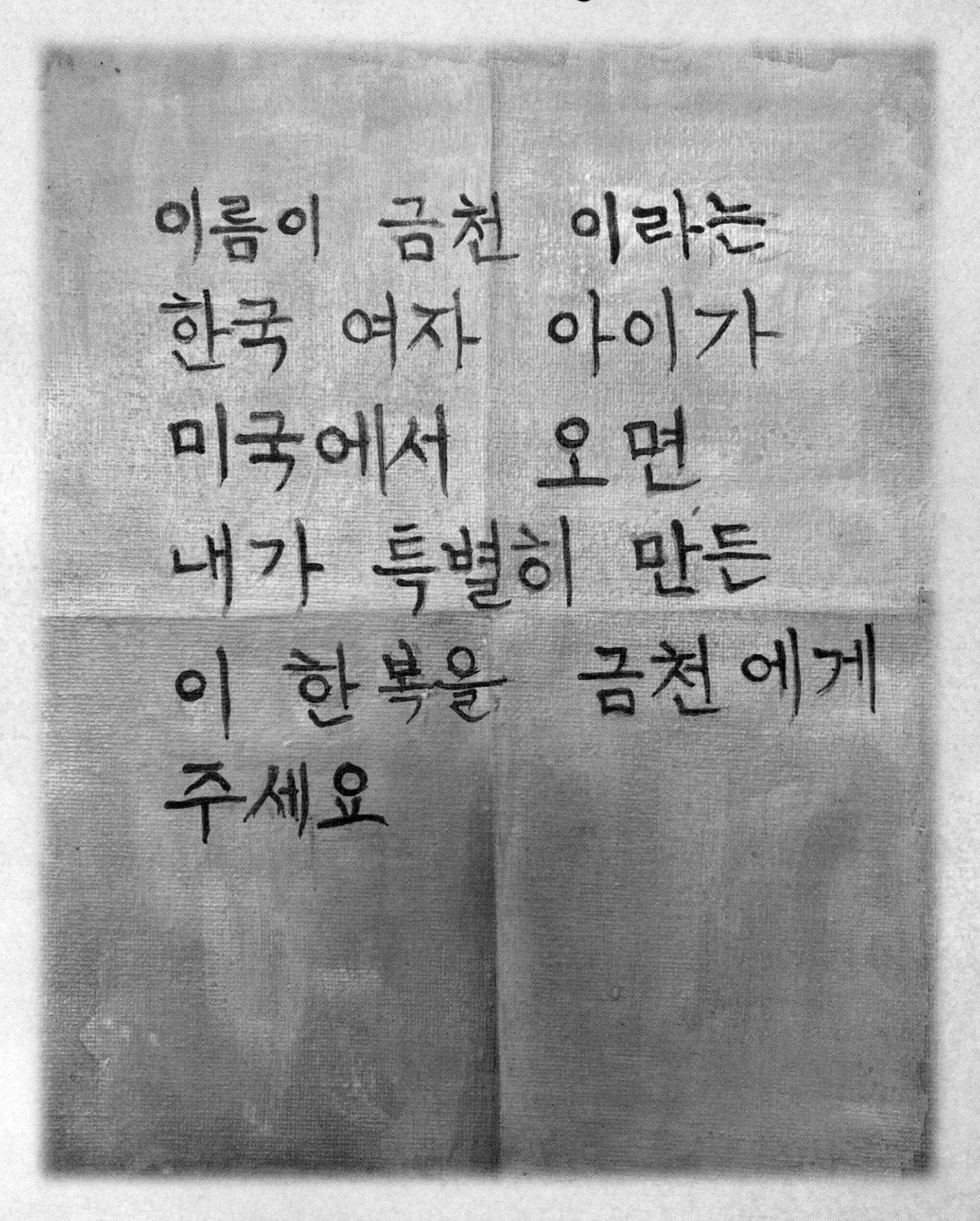
이름이 금천 이라는
한국 여자 아이가
미국에서 오면
내가 특별히 만든
이 한복을 금천에게
주세요

After you were born, she gave you your Korean name and then told your dad and me that we should visit a certain store in Seoul if we ever took you to South Korea.

She never explained why, only that it would make her wish come true."

“Hannah, her wish was for you to have **a beautiful life** in America, but also to not be ashamed of your Korean culture. That’s why it was important to her that you actually went to South Korea yourself to get the dress. By walking in her shoes, you could truly understand the connection between your great-grandma’s journey and your hanbok.

This hanbok represents all of the hard work, bravery, and sacrifice it took for your great-grandma to survive and make a better life for her family and our family.
We wouldn’t be here if it wasn’t for her,” mom explained.

"I wish great-grandma could know that her wish came true," Hannah said quietly. "I wish she was still alive."

"Don't worry," said mom. "I think great-grandma knows you found the hanbok and the hanbok found you, somehow."

When the car pulled up to the school, Hannah's eyes were shining.

She gathered her skirt, grabbed her fans, and kissed her mom. Then she smiled. "I guess life is full of moments to step forward, just like great-grandma used to say.

See you at the talent show!" she yelled as she ran to the auditorium.

As Hannah took the stage, the stage lights caused her dress to sparkle like a **thousand twinkling lights.**

The moment felt magical, like Hannah was always meant to perform, wearing this hanbok. With a crash of the gong, the music started and she began to twirl. She could feel the drumbeats go through her whole body as she flicked her fans to the rhythm.

Snap! Open.

Snap! Closed.

Feathers and glitter from her fans floated around her as she spun faster and faster.

The audience could not take their eyes off her.

When she finished, the clapping and cheers were so loud, she wondered if great-grandma could hear them. She couldn't stop grinning. Mom, dad, grandma, and grandpa were on their feet. Layla, Reena, and Nolan all ran out from backstage, and surrounded her with hugs. With the applause still ringing in her ears, she gave the audience one more twirl and bow, her skirt billowing around her. Hannah had never felt so confident in her life.

The girl named Gold Dress finally felt like her name belonged to her.

She couldn't wait
until the next time
she could step
forward in her
special hanbok
dress.

About the Author

Christine Paik still remembers the butterflies in the pit of her stomach as she performed traditional Korean fan dances as a 12-year-old growing up in Southern California. She never dreamed that over 30 years later, she would be channeling her inner fan dancer to write Hannah's story. Christine is a second generation Korean American wife and mother of two, living in San Diego.

Christine loves telling stories for a living, which started with a 15-year career in TV news and continues today in public relations. She is the winner of six news Emmys and multiple PR awards. She was always an avid reader, but wished there were more Asian American book characters she could relate to (besides Claudia Kishi from *The Babysitter's Club*). So she decided to create her own! Christine also enjoys singing karaoke, photography, and baking.

You can learn more about Christine at www.christinepaik.com.

About the Illustrator

Jung Lin Park never imagined her artwork would ever be published, especially after leaving Ewha Women's University to get married and immigrate from Seoul, Korea to Barstow, California in 1975. She put her artistic aspirations aside to raise her three children and pursue the American dream as a small business owner. She is now the proud grandmother of four grandsons, Luke, Levi, Elias, and Isaiah, and one granddaughter, Sydney, whose hanbok inspired this story.

Recently retired, Lin has started painting in earnest again, at which point her daughter, Christine, approached her with the book idea.
She lives in Southern California with her husband in Christ of 45 years, Hyon Joon Park. When she's not painting, she's sewing, gardening at home, or volunteering at her church.